Buy to Flip Property & Rehab Properties with Florida FL Real Estate

A house flipping business plan & How to Finance a flip property

By Brian Mahoney

Table of Contents

Chapter 1   Buy to Flip Property

Chapter 2   House Flipping Business Plan

Chapter 3   Finding Wholesale priced Investments with buy to flip Property

Chapter 4   How to finance a flip property with 4,000 sources for money!

Chapter 5   How to start flipping houses with no money

Chapter 6   Secrets to getting real estate grants

Chapter 7   Best way to Rehab Real Estate Rehab House

Chapter 8   How to Sell Your Property Fast!

Chapter 9   Insurance for Small Business

Chapter 10   Millionaire Real Estate Rolodex

Chapter 11 Reach a Billion People with Free YouTube Real Estate Marketing

Chapter 12 Florida FL Real Estate

DEDICATION

**This book is dedicated to my son's
Christian and Matthew.
A blessing from God and the joy of my life.**

ACKNOWLEDGMENTS

I WOULD LIKE TO ACKNOWLEDGE ALL THE HARD WORK OF THE MEN AND WOMEN OF THE UNITED STATES MILITARY, WHO RISK THEIR LIVES ON A DAILY BASIS, TO MAKE THE WORLD A SAFER PLACE.

Disclaimer

This book was written as a guide to starting a business. As with any other high yielding action, starting a business has a certain degree of risk. This book is not meant to take the place of accounting, legal, financial or other professional advice. If advice is needed in any of these fields, you are advised to seek the services of a professional.

While the author has attempted to make the information in this book as accurate as possible, no guarantee is given as to the accuracy or currency of any individual item. Laws and procedures related to business are constantly changing.

Therefore, in no event shall Brian Mahoney or MahoneyProducts Publishers be liable for any special, indirect, or consequential damages or any damages whatsoever in connection with the use of the information herein provided.

Chapter 1
Buy to Flip
Property

Buy to Flip Property

House Flipping is a type of real estate investment strategy in which an investor purchases properties with the goal of reselling them for a profit. Profit is generated by purchasing a property well under market value, through the property appreciation in a good housing market or from renovations and capital improvements that increase the value of the investment.

If you want to use the House Flipping real estate investment strategy there a few things you need to do to be successful.

1. Get Knowledge

"My people are destroyed for lack of knowledge..." Hosea 4:6

This book is a beginning. Throughout this book there will be links placed for you to get more education. In addition, there is a web Rolodex resource section near the end this book, that has more real estate sources to bolster your education.

The "Real Estate Terms" section at the end of this book will also help in getting you caught up to the real estate lingo used by real estate professionals.

Buy to Flip Property

2. Secure Financing

I was at a real estate seminar and the instructor asked "what's worth more, a house worth $100,000 or $100,000 cash"? Many people in the audience said "The house. It will appreciate in value." The instructor replied "The $100,000 in cash. With that I can buy the house." If you are going to be an investor, the first thing you need to do is know where or how you are going to finance your business.

You are going to need money to purchase a property and to repair it. There are several sources for funding.

* Your personal savings

* A credit card

* Bank loan

* Hard & Private Money Lenders

* Partners

* Investors

* Family and Friends

There will be More funding details in later chapters.

Buy to Flip Property

3. Begin with the end in mind.

Write a business plan. Set a budget. Choose a specialty.

Begin with the end in mind. A business plan helps you to chart a course of action. Having a business plan can also help you to secure money from a financial institution.

Set a budget. People who lose money in real estate either don't have a budget or don't stick to one. A friend once asked me to finance a property. I asked for the address. I looked at the property and the asking price. Within 24 hours I found a property in the same area that was %50 less and equal in quality. I found that property in part because I had a budget set, and was not willing to go over it. Other people will be more than happy to spend your money and tell you what you can afford. You need to know what you can and can't afford before you get started.

Buy to Flip Property

Choose a specialty. There are plenty to choose from...

* Residential Property

* Commercial Property

* Apartments

* Duplexes

* 3 bedroom homes

* Mobile Homes

* Government Properties

* Bank Properties

* Probate Properties

Learn all you can about a real estate niche, and stick to it until you become very proficient.

Buy to Flip Property

4. Find a great property.

One of the reasons finding a property at a great wholesale price is possible is because many people skip step 2: securing financing. When I was purchasing properties from the government, I learned that cash had priority in many of the deals, even if I was offering less than the asking price.

Risk is a necessary component of success. Purchasing from the government is a great way to get started because there is less risk involved. There are weasels in every business. In general the government is less interested in making a profit and more concerned with getting rid of a non performing asset.

Moving a non-performing asset, is also the same mindset for many banks. There is less emotional value attached to a property as opposed to buying from a regular home owner.

Part of finding a great property is reducing risk. Sticking with the government or banks might reduce your profit, but if you are new to real estate investing, then it is good to get a couple of deals under your belt to build confidence and gain experience.

Buy to Flip Property

5. Put Together a Team

Your team should include but not be limited to...

* a few experienced real estate agents

* a few good contractors and sub-contractors

* a good place to puchase supplies

* a real estate attorney

* a title company

* an accountant

There is enough basic information here to get you started, but we are going to cover in more detail many of the topics mentioned in this introduction.

I once purchased a 3 bedroom house from the government for $1,500. Recently a bank sold me a 5 bedroom house for under $10,000 with a .6 acre (that's the size of an NFL Football Field) back yard in a quiet neighborhood.

Was it Luck?

Buy to Flip Property

"Luck Is What Happens When **Preparation** Meets Opportunity"

Seneca

While I was taking classes and running an online business, I spent 3 hours a day, 5 days a week going through real estate web sites looking for deals.

If you are serious about making money in real estate then treat real estate investing like a business not a hobbie. Part time effort produces part time results.

The longest journey begins with one step.

"Inch by inch, life's a cinch. Yard by yard, life's hard."

— John Bytheway

Chapter 2

House Flipping Business Plan

House Flipping Business Plan

Millions of people want to know what is the secret to making money. Most have come to the conclusion that it is to start a business. So how to start a business? The first thing you do to start is business is to create a business plan.

A business plan is a formal statement of a set of business goals, the reasons they are believed attainable, and the plan for reaching those goals. It may also contain background information about the organization or team attempting to reach those goals.

A professional business plan consists of eight parts.

1. Executive Summary

The executive summary is a very important part of your business plan. Many consider it the most important because it this part of your plan gives a summary of the current state of your business, where you want to take it and why the business plan you have made will be a success. When requesting funds to start your business, the executive summary is an chance to get the attention of a possible investor.

House Flipping Business Plan

2. Company Description

The company description part of your business plan gives a high level review of the different aspects of your business. This is like putting your elevator pitch into a brief summary that can help readers and possible investors quickly grasp the goal of your business and what will make it stand out, or what unique need it will fill.

3. Market Analysis

The market analysis part of your business plan should go into detail about your industries market and monetary potential. You should demonstrate detailed research with logical strategies for market penetration. Will you use low prices or high quality to penetrate the market?

4. Organization and Management

The Organization and Management section follows the Market Analysis. This part of the business plan will have your companies organizational structure, the type of business structure of incorporation, the ownership, management team and the qualifications of everyone holding these positions including the board of directors if necessary.

House Flipping Business Plan

5. Service or Product Line

The Service or Product Line part of your business plan gives you a chance to describe your service or product. Focus on the benefits to the customers more than what the product or service does. For example, a air conditioner makes cold air. The benefit of the product is it cools down and makes customers more comfortable whether they are driving in bumper to bumper traffic or are sick and sitting in a nursing home. Air Conditioners fill a need that could mean the difference between life and death. Use this section to state what are the most important benefits of your product or service and what need it fills.

6. Marketing and Sales

Having a proven marketing plan is essential element to the success of any business. Today online sales are dominating the marketplace. Present a strong internet marketing plan as well as social media plan. YouTube videos, Facebook Ads and Press Releases all can be part of your internet marketing plan. Passing out flyers and business cards are still an effective way to reach potential customers.

Use this part of your business plan to state your projected sales and how you came to that number. Do your research on similar companies for possible statistics on sales numbers.

House Flipping Business Plan

7. Funding Request

When you write your Funding Request section of your business plan, be sure to be detailed and have documentation of the cost of supplies, building space, transportation, overhead and promotion of your business.

8. Financial Projections

The following is a list of the important financial statements to include in your business plan packet.

Historical Financial Data

Your historical financial data would be bank statements, balance sheets and possible collateral for your loan.

Prospective Financial Data

The prospective financial data section of your business plan should show your potential growth within your industry, projecting out for at least the next five years.

You can have monthly or quarterly projections for the first year. Then project from year to year.

Include a ratio and trend analysis for all of your financial statements. Use colorful graphs to explain positive trends, as part of the financial projections section of your business plan.

House Flipping Business Plan

Appendix

The appendix should not be part of the main body of your business plan. It should only be provided on a need to know basis. Your business plan may be seen by a lot of people and you don't want certain information available to everybody. Lenders may need such information so you should have an appendix ready just in case.

The appendix would include:

Credit history (personal & business)

    Resumes of key managers

    Product pictures

    Letters of reference

    Details of market studies

    Relevant magazine articles or book references

    Licenses, permits or patents

    Legal documents

    Copies of leases

House Flipping Business Plan

Building permits

Contracts

List of business consultants, including attorney and accountant

Keep a record of who you allow to see your business plan.

Include a Private Placement Disclaimer. A Private Placement Disclaimers is a private placement memorandum (PPM) is a document focused mainly on the possible downsides of an investment.

CHAPTER 3

Finding Wholesale priced Investments with buy to flip Property

How To Find Wholesale Real Estate

There are several basic methods to find real estate at wholesale prices. There are foreclosures and pre-foreclosures, so get excited! There are hundreds of great deals just waiting for you to find them! The first method is Searching Public Records.

Searching Public Records

Go to your county's recorders office and look for notice of default or notice of sale. The advantage of this method is that many newly posted properties have not been seen by your competition. The disadvantage is that it usually takes more time to find property than the other methods.

Here is a tip. When ever a county clerk helps you, get that person's name and thank them face to face. Then go home and call the office and thank them again. Wait about a week. Then purchase a thank you card and mail it. Your kindness is going to stand out to that clerk. In turn that clerk is not likely to forget you. You in turn will likely have an ally in that office. The old saying "It's not what you know, but who you know." This method helps the clerk and yourself get to know each other quicker than usual. At the very least, you should feel good for being a nice person!

How To Find Wholesale Real Estate

Another advantage to searching public records is Probate Properties. You will need to be educated in your local area's probate laws to purchase those properties.

Probate is required for all estates that are not protected by a trust. The average duration of probate is 7 to 8 months.

If the house is owned outright, the estate is responsible for remitting property taxes and insurance premiums throughout the probate process.

Estate administrators can elect to sell the property if it is causing financial harm to the estate. If the estate does not have sufficient funds to cover outstanding debts, the probate judge can order the property sold.

How a probate house is sold depends on the type of probate that is used. "Court Confirmation" is the most common type of probate used. A judge must approve all of the aspects of the management of the estate. Independent Administration of Estate's Act (IAEA) governs the 2nd type of probate administration. It allows estate executors to engage in estate administrative affairs without the court management.

How To Find Wholesale Real Estate

To purchase probate property you have to know which probate system is being applied. Properties can be bought directly from the estate executor when Independent Administration of Estate's process is in effect. You can place your bid through the court system when court approval is required.

An investor interested in finding probate real estate must research public records. When people pass away their last will and testament is recorded in the probate court. The last will and testament will contain valuable information such as the estate assets, who is the beneficiary, and contact info for whoever is administrating for the estate.

Property records should show if there are any liens on the property and if so, who holds the lien. They should also show the properties appraised value, the year it was constructed, the square footage and the lot size. The records may also help you to determine if there have been any tax liens placed on the property.

Do your due diligence when purchasing any type of real estate. Bring in professional help in the form of building inspectors, lawyers and any other professionals that can help protect you when needed.

How To Find Wholesale Real Estate

Using the Internet

I will provide you with a Small Real Estate Rolodex of web sites later in this chapter. Many are completely free and have tons of information. One success algorithm for buying a property is that you should never, never, purchase one property without looking at, at least 100 other properties. Being able to search online makes using this formula very easy.

Using Local Papers and Journals

Local papers and journals. By law many foreclosures have to be posted in the local paper. This can mean a goldmine of opportunity for you. With newspaper circulation in decline, many people are simply not looking in the newspaper anymore. Advantage you.

Next I am going to cover several categories of real estate sources.

* Nationwide banks & Foreclosure Properties

* Government Foreclosure Properties

* Commercial Real Estate

* FSBO - For Sale By Owner

How To Find Wholesale Real Estate

Nationwide Banks & Foreclosure Properties

Bank of America

http://foreclosures.bankofamerica.com/

I have purchased property using this web site. It is my favorite because they have a large nationwide inventory and their web site is easy to navigate and sort properties.

Wells Fargo

https://reo.wellsfargo.com/

Place yourself on their mailing list, and get property updates on a monthly basis.

Ocwen Financial Corporation

http://www.ocwen.com/reo

Founded in 1988 they are one of the largest mortgage companies in America.

How To Find Wholesale Real Estate

Hubzu

http://www.hubzu.com/

Hubzu is a nationwide real estate auction web site. Very easy to use. This is a great web site for comparing property prices nationwide.

How To Find Wholesale Real Estate

Government Foreclosure Properties

One advantage purchasing from the government is that there is no emotional attachment to the property. Don't be afraid to make a offer that is lower than the listed price. I once argued with a real estate agent who refused to place a offer lower than the stated price. Eventually I got him to place the offer. (Remember that they work for you, however some government properties can't be purchased unless you go through a HUD or government approved agent.) It was countered twice, before I decided to purchase another property. But they countered with two offers lower than the listed price.

If you are reading a ebook version of this book then you should be able to access these web sites by clicking the links below. But if you are reading a paperback version of this book then be careful when looking for government properties. There are many web sites pretending to be government web sites and some will attempt to charge you fees for information about government properties.

How To Find Wholesale Real Estate

Government Foreclosure Properties

Fannie Mae
The Federal National Mortgage Association

https://www.fanniemae.com/singlefamily/reo-vendors

Department of Housing and Urban Development

https://www.hudhomestore.com/Home/Index.aspx

The Federal Deposit Insurance Corporation

https://www.fdic.gov/buying/owned/

The United States Department of Agriculture

https://properties.sc.egov.usda.gov/resales/index.jsp

United States Marshals

https://www.usmarshals.gov/assets/sales.htm#real_estate

How To Find Wholesale Real Estate

Commercial Real Estate Properties

City Feet

is a nationwide database of Commercial Real Estate Property

http://www.cityfeet.com/#

The Commercial Real Estate Listing Service

is a nationwide database of Commercial Real Estate Property

https://www.cimls.com/

Land . Net

is a nationwide database of land, commercial real estate for sale and for lease.

http://www.land.net/

Loop . Net

is a nationwide database of Commercial Real Estate Property

http://www.loopnet.com/

How To Find Wholesale Real Estate

FSBO – For Sale By Owner

By Owner

http://www.byowner.com/

For sale by owner in Canada

http://www.fsbo-bc.com/

For sale by owner Central

http://www.fsbocentral.com/

For sale by Owner: world's largest FSBO web site

http://www.forsalebyowner.com/

Ranch by owner

http://www.ranchbyowner.com/

CHAPTER 4

How to finance a flip property with 4,000 sources for money!

FINANCING REAL ESTATE

Welcome to Expert financing. I am going to show you several realistic ways to finance real estate. You are going to learn how to finance real estate with.

* VA LOANS

* PARTNERS

* INVESTMENT CLUBS

* CREDIT CARDS

* CORPORATE CREDIT

* EQUITY

* SELLER FINANCE

* HARD MONEY LENDERS

* AND FINALLY I SHOW YOU THE MONEY$!!

USING A VA LOAN

According to the web sites www.benefits.va.gov and www.military.com the current VA Loan amount is a whopping $417,000! What a lot of veterans don't know is that you can use that money to purchase not only your home, but investment properties. That is how I started my investing career. Purchasing multiple homes using my VA Loan.

FINANCING REAL ESTATE

Even if you are not a veteran, you can still partner up with one, who still has some money left on his or her VA LOAN.

If you are a Veteran, you will need to obtain a copy of your DD 214 and VA Form 26-1880 Request for a Certificate of Eligibility.

PARTNERS

This is another way I purchased a home. At the time I worked for the United States Postal Service. I had already purchased plenty of homes, so many of the workers were aware I had successfully invested in real estate. At break time I went around and ask people to partner up with me. I had multiple people offer to go in as a partner. I choose one and that house we rehabbed and flipped just two months after purchasing it. To this day it was the biggest gross profit on one deal, I have had. True I had to split it with my partner, but I would rather have half of something than all of nothing.

Having the combined resources of two people can be a great benefit, but it is not without it's challenges. If you are going to use a partner, no matter how close you are...GET EVERY THING IN WRITING.

FINANCING REAL ESTATE

Having a partner can dramatically increase the chance of a Bank lending money as well as having someone to split the work on rehabbing, should you decide to save money and make repairs yourself. But all this must be spelled out BEFORE you enter into a Agreement/Contract and purchase a home.

It helps if the person is like minded and understands the risks and benefits of investing, and truly understands the return on investment of a particular deal.

REAL ESTATE INVESTMENT CLUBS

Real estate investment clubs are groups that meet locally and allow investors and other professionals to network and learn. They can provide extremely useful information for both the novice and expert real estate investor. A top real estate club can provide a great forum to network, learn about reputable contractors, brokers, realtors, lawyers, accountants and other professionals. On the other hand, there are many real estate clubs designed to sell you. They bring in "gurus" who sell either on stage or at the back of the room, and as a result, the clubs typically profit to the tune of %50 of the sale price of the product, bootcamp, or training that is pitched.

FINANCING REAL ESTATE

I have purchased a ton of real estate books and real estate courses. Carlton Sheets, Dave Del Dotto, The Mylands, Seminar courses and much much more. I am not against any club bringing in a speaker who has a course. However I think there should be transparency to the members of the club.

There is certainly value in the networking that may come at one of these groups. But attend working to attain your goals and not necessarily the club's goal to sell you something. Some times both are the same thing. As a rule I usually leave debit cards at home the first time I attend an event. If there is a seller there with a "This day only offer" then I won't feel pressured to purchase. Plus most sellers can be convinced to sell at the discount offer price at a later time when you have had a chance to come down off the "sense of urgency emotional pitch" .

CREDIT CARDS

When using a credit card in real estate you must really do your homework on the deal. Dan Kennedy a world famous marketer once said "always stack the numbers in your favor". That's how you use a credit card. Look at the return on investment as compared to the long term cost of using a credit card and it's interest. Also I would recommend buying low cost homes that you can purchase and own free and clear.

FINANCING REAL ESTATE

No Mortgage Payment!!! My last 2 homes I have purchased have been cash deals. One home cost $1,500 and the other about $7,000. The first was a government property from HUD and the 2nd From a Bank. These institutions are unemotional about real estate and simply view a property as a non performing asset. The 2nd home was 4 bedrooms, 1 1/2 bath and a basement located in a farming community and came with a 2 car garage/shed and   .6 acre(that is the size of a NFL football field) of land.

In this book I show you how to find plenty of houses with amazing below wholesale prices and a formula for almost always finding a great deal.

CORPORATE CREDIT

Many people set up corporations to buy and sell real estate as an additional protection against liabilities. Other's create a corporation to mask personal involvement in property transfers and public records. Regardless of the use of a corporation, you can buy real estate with corporate credit as an alternative to using your own cash or IRA. By capitalizing on the credit rating of your corporation, you can buy real estate and build your corporate holdings portfolio.

FINANCING REAL ESTATE

Just remember that you can set up your corporation in a state that favors you the most for your real estate deals. Do your research. Most people like Delaware and Nevada, but you will have to decide if your home state or any other state is best for you and your business.

CURRENT EQUITY

Using the equity in your home for real estate investing is another way you can finance properties. You might use the money for a down payment or it may only be enough to cover the cost of some rehab repairs.

If you stick to the low cost home formula, you may have enough to purchase the entire house. A house is an investment that should appreciate in value as well as give a great ROI (Return On Investment). When you decide to flip the property or rent it out for positive cashflow.

If you have equity and it's not doing anything, then you may decide to make it a "performing asset" and use it as part of your real estate finance program.

FINANCING REAL ESTATE

SELLER FINANCING

Seller finance is where the seller of a free and clear property becomes your bank along with being the seller.

Advantages:

You get to purchase the property on terms that may be more beneficial for you. Seller gets monthly payments and the benefit of treating the sale as an installment sale thus allowing them to defer any capital gains taxes that may be due.

Disadvantages:

You may be locked into a mortgage with a pre-payment penalty or may not be able to resell the property immediately. This strategy is typically not meant for flipping but can definitely be used for that purpose if structured correctly.

Seller Finance is a known way to finance a property. That is why I have presented it in this book. But it is my least favorite because you now have a lingering relationship with your property. Your ability to make decisions regarding the property is limited and for that reason, I would not go this route. However, like all types of financing, you have to ask yourself, "is the deal worth it."

FINANCING REAL ESTATE

I also prefer to work alone, but when a great deal came along, I sought out a partner to make it happen. Risk is usually relative to potential profit.

HARD MONEY LENDERS

A hard money lender is usually a individual or company that lends money for an investment secured by the investment property.

Advantages:

Less red tape to get the money. You are dealing with people who understand the real estate investment business.

Disadvantage:

This is not a long term loan. The lender wants a return on investment, usually within a few months, a a year, or a few years. The interest rate on the loan is much higher than usual conventional banks.

Using hard money has a higher risk because the return on investment is due quicker. Therefore it is a good idea not to use a Hard Money Lender, until you have a great deal of experience and confidence in being able to produce a return on investment.

SHOWING YOU THE MONEY

A list of web sites for financing.

www.businessfinance.com (4,000 sources of money!)

www.advanceamericaproperty.com

http://www.cashadvanceloan.com/

www.brookviewfinancial.com

www.commercialfundingcorp.com

www.dhlc.com
(hard money for the Texas area)

www.equity-funding.com

www.bankofamerica.com

www.carolinahardmoney.com
(for real estate investors in North and South Carolina)

www.fpfloans.com

FINANCING REAL ESTATE

As you can see there are plenty of strategies for financing a property. Do your research on your investment property and get the true market value. Purchase well below wholesale. This will help to minimize risk and elevate your potential profit margins. Buying below wholesale also creates a buffer for unexpected expenses.

So don't let the lack of money be a roadblock in your real estate investing dreams.

Chapter 5

How to start flipping houses with no money

How to Start Flipping Houses with No Money

In 2015 over $34 billion dollars was raised by crowdfunding. Crowdfunding and Crowdsourcing roots began in 2005 and they help to finance or fund projects by raising money from a large number of people, usually by using the internet.

This type of fundraising or venture capital usually has 3 components. The individual or organization with a project that needs funding, groups of people who donate to the project, and a organization sets up a structure or rules to put the two together.

These websites do charge fees. The standard fee for success is about %5. If your goal is not met there is also a fee.

Below is a list of the top Crowdfunding websites according to myself and Entrepreneur Magazine Contributor Sally Outlaw.

How to Start Flipping Houses with No Money

https://www.indiegogo.com/

Started as a platform for getting movies made, now helps to raise funds for any cause.

http://rockethub.com/

Started as a platform for the arts, now it helps to raise funds for business, science, social projects and education.

http://peerbackers.com/

Peerbackers focuses on raising funds for business, entrepreneurs and innovators.

https://www.kickstarter.com/

The most popular and well know n of all the crowdfunding websites. Kickstarter focuses on film, music, technology, gaming, design and the creative arts. Kickstarter only accepts projects from the United States, Canada and the United Kingdom.

How to Start Flipping Houses with No Money

Group Growvc

http://group.growvc.com/

This website is for business and technology innovation.

https://microventures.com/

Get access to angel investors. This website is for business startups.

https://angel.co/

Another website for business startups.

https://circleup.com/

Circle up is for innovative consumer companies.

https://www.patreon.com/

If you start a YouTube Channel (highly recommended) you will hear about this website frequently. This website is for creative content people.

How to Start Flipping Houses with No Money

https://www.crowdrise.com/

"Raise money for any cause that inspires you." The Landing page slogan speaks for itself. #1 fundraising website for personal causes.

https://www.gofundme.com/

This fundraising website allows for business, charity, education, emergencies, sports, medical, memorials, animals, faith, family, newlyweds etc...

https://www.youcaring.com/

The leader in free fundraising. Over $400 million raised.

https://fundrazr.com/

FundRazr is an award-winning online fundraising platform that has helped thousands of people and organizations raise money
for causes they care about.

Chapter 6

Secrets to Getting Real Estate Grants

How to write a Winning Grant Proposal

Secrets to Getting Real Estate Grants

Government grants. Many people either don't believe government grants exist or they don't think they would ever be able to get government grant money.

First lets make one thing clear. Government grant money is **YOUR MONEY**. Government money comes from taxes paid by residents of this country. Depending on what state you live in, you are paying taxes on almost everything....Property tax for your house. Property tax on your car. Taxes on the things you purchase in the mall, or at the gas station. Taxes on your gasoline, the food you buy etc.

So get yourself in the frame of mind that you are not a charity case or too proud to ask for help, because billionaire companies like GM, Big Banks and most of Corporate America is not hesitating to get their share of **YOUR MONEY**!

There are over two thousand three hundred (2,300) Federal Government Assistance Programs. Some are loans but many are formula grants and project grants. To see all of the programs available go to:

https://beta.sam.gov/help/assistance-listing

Secrets to Getting Real Estate Grants

The Basic Components of a Proposal

There are eight basic components to creating a solid proposal package:

1. The proposal summary;

2. Introduction of organization;

3. The problem statement   (or needs assessment);

4. Project objectives;

5. Project methods or design;

6. Project evaluation;

7. Future funding; and

8. The project budget.

Secrets to Getting Real Estate Grants

The Proposal Summary

The Proposal Summary is an outline of the project goals and objectives. Keep the Proposal Summary short and to the point. No more that 2 or 3 paragraphs. Put it at the beginning of the proposal.

Introduction

The Introduction portion of your grant proposal presents you and your business as a credible applicant and organization.

Highlight the accomplishments of your organization from all sources: newspaper or online articles etc. Include a biography of key members and leaders. State the goals and philosophy of the company.

The Problem Statement

The problem statement makes clear the problem you are going to solve(maybe reduce homelessness). Make sure to use facts. State who and how those affected will benefit from solving the problem. State the exact manner in how you will solve the problem.

Secrets to Getting Real Estate Grants

Project Objectives

The Project Objectives section of your grant proposal focuses on the Goals and Desired outcome.

Make sure to indentify all objectives and how you are going to reach these objectives. The more statistics you can find to support your objectives the better. Make sure to put in realistic objectives. You may be judged on how well you accomplish what you said you intended to do.

Program Methods and Design

The program methods and design section of your grant proposal is a detailed plan of action.

What resources are going to be used.

What staff is going to be needed.

System development.

Create a Flow Chart of project features.

Explain what will be achieved.

Try to produce evidence of what will be achieved.

Make a diagram of program design.

Secrets to Getting Real Estate Grants

Evaluation

There is product evaluation and process evaluation. The product evaluation deals with the result that relate to the project and how well the project has met it's objectives.

The process evaluation deals with how the project was conducted, how did it line up with the original stated plan and the overall effectiveness of the different aspects of the plan.

Evaluations can start at anytime during the project or at the project's conclusion. It is advised to submit a evaluation design at the start of a project.

It looks better if you have collected convincing data before and during the program.

If evaluation design is not presented at the beginning that might encourage a critical review of the program design.

Future Funding

The Future Funding part of the grant proposal should have long term project planning past the grant period.

Secrets to Getting Real Estate Grants

Budget

Utilities, rental equipment, staffing, salary, food, transportation, phone bills and insurance are just some of the things to include in the budget.

A well constructed budget accounts for every penny.

For a complete guide for government grants google

catalog of federal domestic assistance. You can download a complete PDF version of the catalog.

Other sources of Government Funding

You can get General Small Business loans from the government. Go to the Small Business Administration for more information.

SBA Microloan Program

The Microloan program provides loans of up to $50,000 with the average loan being $13,000.

https://www.sba.gov/

Here are a Few Current Commercial Real Estate

Grant/Loan Programs

Program Number: 10.415

Program Name: Rural Rental Housing Loans

Department: Department of Agriculture

Assistance: Grants - Direct Loans

Program Number: 10.438

Program Name: Section 538 Rural Rental

Department: Department of Agriculture

Assistance: Guaranteed Loans

Program Number: 14.191

Program Name: Multifamily Housing

Department: HUD

Assistance: Project Grants

A Few Current Commercial Real Estate Grant/Loan Programs

Program Number: 14.314

Program Name: Assisted Living Conversion

Department: HUD

Assistance: Project Grants

Program Number: 14.326

Program Name: Rental Assistance 811

Department: HUD

Assistance: Project Grants

Program Number: 14.329

Program Name: HUD Multifamily PSF Pilot

Department: HUD

Assistance: Direct Payments for Specified Use

Secrets to Getting Real Estate Grants

Recently billionaire Elon Musk was awarded 4.9 billion dollars in government subsidies. If you are hesitant to pursue government assistance, let that sink in. A billionaire who pays little in taxes was given billions of your tax dollars.

Government grants are real. Like anything else worthwhile, there is effort and qualifications that must be met to obtain them.

Chapter 7

Best way to Rehab Real Estate Rehab House

Best way to Rehab Real Estate Rehab House

There are three basic components to rehabbing a property. Have a property inspection, a cost analysis and hire a contractor.

A. Home Inspection

You can hire a licensed professional to inspect the propery or you can do it yourself. I advise hiring a licensed professional with a great deal of experience.

To hire a professional you can google "home inspection, your city, your state" or go to homeadvisor.com.

http://www.homeadvisor.com/

https://goo.gl/vL4gWK

If you choose to do it yourself here is a basic home inspection checklist.

Best way to Rehab Real Estate Rehab House

Exterior

* Roof: Determine if the roof needs repairs or needs to be replaced.

* Lawn: Determine what kind of landscaping is needed or if the yard needs to be reseeded.

* Sprinkler: Is there a sprinkler system? If so does it work?

* Lights: Do the lights work? Are there motion sensors? Are there cost efficient bulbs?

* Outlets: Do the outlets work?

* Fence: Does it need repair or painting?

* Trees: Do any trees need to be removed or trimmed?

* Garage Door: Does it open and close easily?

Best way to Rehab Real Estate Rehab House

Overall Interior

* **Walls:** Do they need paint or repair?

* **Floors:** Do tiles or carpet need to be replaced? Do wood floors need to be repaired?

* **Stairs:** Are the stairs sturdy? Do they make noise. Is the handrail sturdy and safe?

***Outlets:** Purchase a voltage tester and see if all the outlets work.

* **Doors:** Do they open and close easily? Are they level?

***Windows:** Do you feel any breezes when you stand by them? Are they cost efficient?

***Lights:** Turn on every light switch to make sure they work. (Note: If the home is unoccupied and the power is turned off, this won't be possible.)

Best way to Rehab Real Estate Rehab House

Kitchen

* **Countertops:** Check for chips and cracks.

* **Cabinets:** Do they open and close easily? Do they need to be refinished or replaced?

* **Oven:** Does the oven work? Is it outdated?

* **Refrigerator:** Check to see if it freezes. Does it pass the eyeball test or is it an eyesore.

* **Faucet:** Run the water in the sink. Any leaks? How is the water pressure?

* **Range Hood:** See if the range hood fan and light work. It most likely will need to be cleaned.

Best way to Rehab Real Estate Rehab House

Bathrooms

* **Plumbing/Drainage:** Fill up the sink and tub and see how the water drains out.

* **Faucets:**   Check for leaks.

* **Toilet:**   Is there enough pressure when it is flushed?

* **Bath Tub:**   Is it too small? Any scratches?

* **Ventilation:**   Does the fan work? Is there a window? Does it open and close easily?

Bedrooms

* **Closets:**   Is there enough space? Are hanger rods needed?

Best way to Rehab Real Estate Rehab House

Living/Dining/Family Room

* Ceiling Fans: Do ceiling fans need to be added or replaced?

Basement

* Mold: If there is an odor, check for mold and mildew.

* Furnace: Does the furnace work? Is it outdated? Up to code?

* Water Heater: Check for water around the base of the water heater. Any stickers on this to indicate installation date?

A documentary about Walt Disney revealed that Walt purchased a home for his parents and a faulty gas furnace was the cause of his mother's death. So inspecting a house can be a life or death matter.

You can use this checklist to determine your offer price and begin a overall cost analysis. However it is highly recommended that you use a professional.

Best way to Rehab Real Estate Rehab House

B. Cost Analysis

When investing in real estate, you should always stack the numbers in your favor. If you can purchase a property at %50 of it's wholesale value, then you leave enough margin for error to absorb expenses and still sell the property for a profit.

The real estate web site biggerpockets.com has a investment calculator that can do the cost analysis work for you.

https://www.biggerpockets.com/real-estate-investment-calculator

https://goo.gl/HFoK9x

Best way to Rehab Real Estate Rehab House

However you can do a quick cost analysis yourself. Here are the basic numbers you will need.

* after repair value

* desired profit

* estimated repair cost

* purchase closing cost

* sale closing cost

* agent commission

* monthly holding costs

* number of days it will take to rehab and sell

Take the "after repair value" and substract all of the expenses.

Best way to Rehab Real Estate Rehab House

C. Hire a Contractor

It is a good idea that you hire a contractor. However if you decide to do the repair work yourself there is a supply discount program from Home Depot.

WHAT IS IT?

You have to get their Pro Xtra Account. If you're spending at least $1,500, chances are you can save money. In select markets, you may only need to spend only $1,000. Check with your local store to confirm required purchase amount.

HOW DOES IT WORK?

Assemble your project list. Build your cart in the store. If your total adds up to at least $1,500 (or $1,000 in select markets, check with your local store), you probably qualify for a volume discount.

Quotes can be processed by the Pro Desk any time and most requests are priced immediately. Membership in Pro Xtra Loyalty Program is required to receive discounts.

Full details are at the web site listed below...

http://www.homedepot.com/c/Pro_VolumePricing

Best way to Rehab Real Estate Rehab House

A. How to Find a good Contractor

Go to your local building material warehouses like Lowes, Home Depot, Menards and Sherwin Williams.

Ask them who are their high volume contractors. If contracters are frequently purchasing supplies then they are frequently working. This is one of the more reliable ways to find a quality contractor.

Ask other contractors. Often times you will come across a good contractor who is busy on another project. Ask him/her for recommendations.

Ask a high volume real estate agent. Top real estate agents usually know one or two good contractors.

Use the internet.

Google "contractors, your city, your state".

Use homeadvisor.com

Try angieslist.com

Best way to Rehab Real Estate Rehab House

B. Contractor Checklist

Hiring the right contractor can make or break a deal. Remember they work for you, so don't be shy about asking questions and getting proof, BEFORE you sign a contract. Here is a question checklist.

1. Do you have a license bond and insurance?

Do You Carry General Liability Insurance?

- It is Best to find a remodel contractor that carries general liability insurance.

2. Do you have referrals?

Do not hesitate to call referrals. - Nice to get several customer references from the last 6 months to one year.

3. Can I get a detailed and comprehensive scope of work with the bid?

4. Ask about experience and verify if you can.

Best way to Rehab Real Estate Rehab House

5. Who's doing the work and who's going to be the daily contact on the project?

- Make sure the contractor or his foreman is on the job whenever work is being performed.

6. Will You Pull All the Required Building Permits?

- Pulling the required building permits, you know things will be done to "code."

7. Do You Guarantee Your Work?

Your contractor should guarantee his work for at least one year from date of completion. They should also include any warranties from the material used if applicable.

8. How do you handle clean up?

Clean up can be expensive. You need to know if the best options are being used.

Best way to Rehab Real Estate Rehab House

9. How Is Payment Handled?

- Per job?

- Upon completion?

- Weekly?

- Some money upfront?

- Do you have capital to buy materials in case we need you to?

These are basic questions that you should be asking to interview contractors before you begin any job. Hiring the right contractor can go a long way in giving you peace of mind, when you are a Real Estate investor.

Chapter 8

HOW TO SELL YOUR PROPERTY FAST!

12 Steps to Selling Any Property Fast!

HOW TO SELL YOUR PROPERTY FAST!

12 Steps to Selling Any Property Fast!

1. Clean and Paint the house

Make sure the house is clean and uncluttered. This makes it easier for a buyer to envision themselves living there. Make the bathrooms and kitchen a priority.

2. Scent the house

You might use a light incent or get some vanilla extract and place it on a old school lightbulb to give it a fresh baked cookie smell.

3. Write a property description

Writing a great property description is key to getting buyers interested in your home. One short cut to learning how to write a good property description is to view property listings of sold properties.

4. Take Good pictures

If you don't have a good camera, buy one. A picture is worth a 1,000 words.

HOW TO SELL YOUR PROPERTY FAST!

12 Steps to Selling Any Property Fast!

5. Send a email to your buyers list

If you do not have a buyer's list, here is a link to a complete set of training videos on how to build a valuable customer list.

https://urlzs.com/6Q2uQ

6. Post ads on craigslist

Keep reposting your ads on a daily basis so that you stay at the top of the search results.

7. Post ads to Backpage

http://www.backpage.com/

This is a Worldwide Classified Ad Web Site.

HOW TO SELL YOUR PROPERTY FAST!

12 Steps to Selling Any Property Fast!

8. Place a Ad on http://realeflow.com/

This is the number one source for real estate investing leads.

9. visit the zillow rental manager https://www.zillow.com/rental-manager/

This is a free rental web site.

10. Create a video virtual tour

Create a video virtual tour and upload the video to YouTube. This is a powerful tool. YouTube is 2nd only to Google as the largest Search Engine in the world. However just posting a video won't get it seen. It has to be Search Engine Optimized(SEO). Below is a link to training videos that will show you step by step how to create great videos and get massive traffic viewing them!

https://urlzs.com/6Q2uQ

HOW TO SELL YOUR PROPERTY FAST!

12 Steps to Selling Any Property Fast!

11. Post an ad on facebook target a city

You can place an ad on Facebook and target the city that your property is in.

12. Place a Standard For Sale sign in the yard

If possible have flyers available as well.

13. Place addition white signs in the yard

Give more information and get more attention by placing more personal signs in the yard.

14. List the property in the MLS

If you are not a real estate agent get one to do it for you.

HOW TO SELL YOUR PROPERTY FAST!

12 Steps to Selling Any Property Fast!

15. Place directional signs

Help people find your house. Make sure you are not violating any county codes when placing signs.

16. Continue marketing until closing

Don't slack off. If necessary you might want to hire VA's Virtual Assistants to keep all ads running.

17. Eliminating Negative Cash Flow

https://www.airbnb.com/

Airbnb is a web site that markets your house or rooms in your house for rent. It's easier to sell your house when it is clean, empty and buyers can envision themselves living in it.

However, if you are suffering from negative cash flow you might want to look into just renting out 1 room in the house.

HOW TO SELL YOUR PROPERTY FAST!
12 Steps to Selling Any Property Fast!

In Summary

1. Clean and Paint the house

2. Scent the house

3. Write a property description

4. Take Good pictures

5. Send a email to your buyers list

6. Post ads on craigslist

7. Post ads to http://www.backpage.com/

8. Place a Ad on http://realeflow.com/

9. https://www.zillow.com/rental-manager/

10. Create a video virtual tour

11. Post an ad on facebook target a city

12. Place a Standard For Sale sign in the yard

13. Place addition white signs in the yard

14. List property in the MLS

15. Place directional signs

16. Continue marketing until closing

17. Rent on Airbnb to eliminate negative cashflow

Take these steps to sell your property and you stack the odds in your favor for a quick property sale!

CHAPTER 9

Insurance for Small Business

Insurance for Small Business

Consult an attorney for any and all of your business matters.

In the early 1990's an elderly woman purchased a hot cup of coffee from a McDonald's drive-thru window in Albuquerque. She spilled the coffee, and suffered 3rd degree burns. She sued Mcdonald's and won. She won 2.7 million dollars in a punitive damages victory. The verdict was appealed and settlement is estimated at somewhere in the neighborhood of $500,000 dollars. All because she spilled the coffee into her lap, while trying to add sugar and cream.

Two men in Ohio, were carpet layers. They were severely burned when a three and a half gallon container of carpet adhesive ignited, when the hot water heater it was sitting next to, was turned on. They felt the warning lable on the back of the can was insufficient. So they filed a lawsuit against the adhesive manufacturers and were awarded nine million dollars.

A woman in Oklahoma, purchased a brand new Winnebago. While driving it home, she set the cruise control to 70 miles per hour. She then left the drivers seat to make some coffee or a sandwich in the back of the motor home.

Insurance for Small Business

The vehicle crashed and the woman sued Winnebago for not advising her, that cruise control does not drive and steer the vehicle. She won 1.7 million dollars and the company had to rewrite their instruction manual.

Unfortunately all three outrageous lawsuits are real. If you are going to run a business, any business, you should consider protecting yourself with Professional Liability Insurance, also known as Errors and Omissions (E & 0) insurance.

This type of insurance can help to protect you from having to pay the full cost of defending yourself against a negligence lawsuit claim.

Error and Omissions can protect you against claims that are not usually covered in regular liability insurance. Those policies usually cover bodily harm, or damage to property. Error and Omissions can protect you agaist negligence, and other mental anguish like inaccurate advice, or misrepresentation. Criminal prosecution is not covered.

Errors and Ommision insurance is recommended for notaries public, real estate brokers or investors and professionals like: software engineers, lawyers, home inspectors web site delvelopers and landscape architects to name a few professions.

Insurance for Small Business

The Most Common Errors and Omission Claims:

%25 Breach of Fiduciary Duty

%15 Breach of Contract

%14 Negligence

%13 Failure to Supervise

%11 Unsuitability

%10 Other

Insurance for Small Business

Things you should know about or require before purchasing a Errors and Omission policy is...

* What is the limit of liability

* What is the Deductible

* Does it include FDD First Dollar Defense - which obligates the insurance company to fight a case without a deductible first.

* Do I have Tail-end coverage or Extended Reporting Coverage (insurance that lasts into retirement)

* Extended coverage for Employees

* Cyber Liability Coverage

* Department of Labor Fiduciary Coverage

* Insolvency Coverage

If you get Errors and Omission insurance, renew it the day it expires. You must be careful to avoid gaps in your coverage, or it could result in not getting your policy renewed.

Insurance for Small Business

A few E & O Insurance Providers:

Insureon

Insureon states that their median Errors and Omissions Insurance policy cost about $750 a year or about $65 a month. The price of course will vary according to your business, the policy you choose and other risk factors.

https://www.insureon.com/home

EOforless

EOforless.com helps insurance, investment, and real estate professionals buy E & O insurance at an affordable cost in five minutes or less.

https://www.eoforless.com/

Insurance for Small Business

CalSurance Associates

As a leading insurance broker, CalSurance Associates, a division of Brown & Brown Program Insurance Services, Inc. has over fifty years of experience delivering comprehensive insurance products, exceptional service, and proven results to over 150,000 insured. They provide professionals nationwide and across multiple industries, including some of the largest financial firms and insurance companies in the United States.

http://www.calsurance.com/csweb/index.aspx

Better Safe Than Sorry

Insurance is one of the hidden costs of doing business. These are just a few companies and a brief overview on the topic of business insurance. Make sure to talk to an attorney or quailified insurance agent before making any decision on insurance. Protect you and your business. Many states do not require E & O insurances. But when you see the cost of some of the settlements, it's better to be safe than sorry.

Chapter 10

Millionaire Real Estate Rolodex

Get Started Fast with these Business Web Sites

MILLIONAIRE ROLODEX

As of the writing of this book, all of the companies web site's are up and running. From time to time companies go out of business or change their web address. So, instead of just giving you just 1 source I give you plenty of sources to choose from.

Top 15 Most Popular eBizMBA Rank

Real Estate Websites

with Estimated Unique Monthly Visitors

1. **Zillow**	36,000,000
2. **Trulia**	23,000,000
3. **Yahoo! Homes**	20,000,000
4. **Realtor**	18,000,000
5. **Redfin**	6,000,000
6. **Homes**	5,000,000

MILLIONAIRE ROLODEX

Top 15 Most Popular eBizMBA Rank

Real Estate Websites	Monthly Visitors
7. ApartmentGuide	2,500,000
8. Curbed	2,000,000
9. ReMax	1,800,000
10. HotPads	1,750,000
11. ZipRealty	1,600,000
12. Apartments	1,500,000
13. Rent	1,400,000
14. Auction	1,300,000
15. ForRent	1,200,000

MILLIONAIRE ROLODEX

Nationwide Banks & Foreclosure Properties

Bank of America

http://foreclosures.bankofamerica.com/

Wells Fargo

https://reo.wellsfargo.com/

Ocwen Financial Corporation

http://www.ocwen.com/reo

Hubzu

http://www.hubzu.com/

MILLIONAIRE ROLODEX

Government Foreclosure Properties

Fannie Mae
The Federal National Mortgage Association

https://www.fanniemae.com/singlefamily/reo-vendors

Department of Housing and Urban Development

https://www.hudhomestore.com/Home/Index.aspx

The Federal Deposit Insurance Corporation

https://www.fdic.gov/buying/owned/

The United States Department of Agriculture

https://properties.sc.egov.usda.gov/resales/index.jsp

United States Marshals

https://www.usmarshals.gov/assets/sales.htm#real_estate

MILLIONAIRE ROLODEX

Commercial Real Estate Properties

City Feet

http://www.cityfeet.com/#

The Commercial Real Estate Listing Service

https://www.cimls.com/

Land . Net

http://www.land.net/

Loop . Net

http://www.loopnet.com/

MILLIONAIRE ROLODEX

FSBO – For Sale By Owner Properties

By Owner

http://www.byowner.com/

For sale by owner in Canada

http://www.fsbo-bc.com/

For sale by owner Central

http://www.fsbocentral.com/

For sale by Owner: world's largest FSBO web site

http://www.forsalebyowner.com/

Ranch by owner

http://www.ranchbyowner.com/

MILLIONAIRE ROLODEX

Tools to Get You Started Video Marketing

https://www.YouTube.com/

Upload your videos to this web site.

https://www.wikipedia.org/

Get valuable information for video topics.

https://screencast-o-matic.com/

Use this screen capture software to create videos

http://www.openoffice.org/download/

Use this Open source word processor software to make slides for your videos.

MILLIONAIRE ROLODEX

Free Keyword Tools

Google keyword planner

https://adwords.google.com/home/tools/keyword-planner/

SEO Centro

http://www.seocentro.com/

Ubersuggest

https://ubersuggest.io/

Promoting Your Real Estate/Videos

Top Free Press Release Websites

https://www.prlog.org

https://www.pr.com

https://www.pr-inside.com

https://www.newswire.com

https://www.OnlinePRNews.com

MILLIONAIRE ROLODEX

Top Social Media Websites

https://www.facebook.com

https://www.tumbler.com

https://www.pinterest.com

https://www.reddit.com

https://www.linkedin.com/

http://digg.com/

https://twitter.com

https://instagram.com

For Everything Under the Sun at Wholesale Prices

http://www.liquidation.com/

COMPUTERS/Office Equipment

http://www.wtsmedia.com/

http://www.laptopplaza.com/

http://www.outletpc.com/

MILLIONAIRE ROLODEX

With this "Millionaire Rolodex" of real estate business resources, you have a ton of web sites that you can use to get started working on your real estate business with little to no money.

So take advantage of these resources to continue to gain valuable knowledge, save money and promote your real estate business.

Chapter 11

Reach a Billion People with Free YouTube Real Estate Marketing

YouTube Real Estate Marketing Overview

Million Dollar Video Marketing

When you read the title of this chapter you may have thought the term "Million Dollar" was hyperbole. However the beauty of video marketing is that it can be done for free, and that there really are several people who make millions of dollars just on their YouTube video's alone. Meaning that they allow ads to be placed on them and they get paid a portion of what google gets from businesses that runs the ads.

Since they are only getting a portion of what is being paid, that means if they make a million dollars, the video's actually produced multi-millions of dollars in ad revenue.

Here are a list of YouTube Millionaires as reported by Forbes magazine in the 20 December 2016 issue.

Youtube name/channel	2016 Income
1. Pewdiepie	$15 Million

Makes video's of himself playing video games and making crude comments on girls dancing.

| 2. Atwood | $8 Million |

YouTube Real Estate Marketing Overview

Promotes products and tours with other Youtubers.

   3. Lilly Singh $7.5 Million

Makes comedy skits mostly featuring herself talking about her parents and relationship issues.

YouTube name/channel	2016 Income
4. Smosh	$7 Million
Comedy Duo.	
5. Rosanna Pasino Nerdie Nummies	$6 Million
Baking show	
6. Markipler	$5.5 Million
Comments on Video Games.	
7. German Garmendia	$5.5 Million
Got a publishing deal from his YouTube channel	
8. Miranda Sings	$5 Million
Comedian	

YouTube Real Estate Marketing Overview

9. Collen Ballinger $5 Million

Comedian

10. Tyler Oakley $5 Million

Makes a diary. LGBT Activist

And these are just some the the top earners. There are many more making $50,000 a month talking about movies, how to put on make up or video taping a day at an amusement park.

A Few Keys to Video Marketing Success

1. Commitment

While many of the top YouTubers are funny, they take their business seriously. One of the first things you have to understand is that there is commitment needed to be successful on YouTube.

Many of the successful YouTubers put up video's daily! One such YouTuber is Grace Randolph (Beyond the Trailer). Grace comments on movie news and movie trailers. She typically uploads 1-3 video's a day.

YouTube Real Estate Marketing Overview

2. Research

Just putting up a video will not guarantee views. You have to put in research for every video. Research if the topic is popular or trending. Research what keywords you should use in your video. Research the success of other video's. Skip the research, skip the success.

3. Popularity

There are certain topics on YouTube that are extremely popular. Star Wars, Disney, Scantily clad women, video games, comedy. Know the level of your topics popularity and try to use keyword planning to max out the highest possible level. Some educational material is extremely valuable, but not popular.

ZERO COST MARKETING OVERVIEW

This is a zero cost online marketing plan for any business, cause or idea you wish to promote. This plan will show you step by step how to use online marketing featuring YouTube and Article Marketing to get free advertising for any product. In addition, this chapter will show you how to use this zero cost marketing plan to create a passive income stream.

YouTube Real Estate Marketing Overview

A Few Key Definitions

YouTube is a video-sharing website headquartered in San Bruno, California, United States. The service was created by three former PayPal employee in February 2005. In November 2006, it was bought by Google for 1.65 Billion dollars. According to the Huffington Post, YouTube has 1 billion active users each month. Or nearly one out of every two people on the internet.

AdSense (Google AdSense) is an advertising placement service by Google. The program is designed for website publishers who want to display targeted text, video or image advertisement on website pages and earn money when the site visitors view or click the ads.

Hyperlink is a link from a hypertext file or document to another location or file, typically activated by clicking on a highlighted word or image on the screen.

Black Hat

In search engine optimization (SEO) terminology, black hat SEO refers to the use of aggressive SEO strategies, techniques and tactics that focus only on search engines and not a human audience, and usually does not obey search engines guidelines.

YouTube Real Estate Marketing Overview

Getting Started

You get started by opening up a YouTube account. Go to www.YouTube.com and follow the step by step instructions. Then you open up a AdSense account. The AdSense account will take about a week to open. AdSense is linked to your YouTube account and land bank account. AdSense will use your 9 digit routing number to deposit a small amount of money into your land bank account. You then have to report to AdSense the amount deposited. After the deposit is confirmed, AdSense will send you a postcard to verify your address. You must then report to AdSense the pin number located on the postcard. Once all the verification takes place YouTube allows you to connect all of the accounts and by doing so, you can now monetize your video's and create a passive income stream.

Social Media

You should join Social Media web sites like Facebook, Google Plus, Digg, Twitter, Linkedin, Tumbler and Pinterest. Every time you upload a video. When you are finished Optimizing it, you should link it to all of your social media web sites. This creates Backlinks. A Backlink is an incoming hyperlink from one webpage to another. Google and YouTube will rank your video higher if it has a good number of Backlinks. However if you have too many, and it appears that you have created them artificially, then Google and YouTube can punish you by removing your video.

YouTube Real Estate Marketing Overview

As long as you are backlinking organically and not using Black Hat software or Black Hat web sites, you should be find with Google and YouTube.

Show Me the Money!

Monetization involves you allowing AdSense to place ads that run before or are placed on your videos. If the ads are clicked on, you make money. If the ads are viewed in their entirety you make money.

After you have your accounts set up, you need to gather all of the tools you will be using to create videos. You can create your videos using a standard video camera and tripod and videotape yourself. Or any other number of ways you can capture video. However for this program we are going "zero cost" so there will be no need to purchase or obtain a video camera.

Getting Free Tools to Create Your Videos

We are going to use "Screen Capture" software. Go to http://screencast-o-matic.com/home to download a free screen capture software called Screencast-o-Matic. There are two versions. The Free version allows you to videotape up to 15 minutes of content and places a watermark on all of your recordings. The pro version makes longer recordings and has edit tools and not watermark. The pro version cost $15 a year and may be worth the investment once your business begins to make a profit.

YouTube Real Estate Marketing Overview

Then next tool you will use in creating your videos is a free copy of the office software package called Apache OpenOffice. Go to https://www.openoffice.org/download/ to download the software.

100% Copyright Free Content

Now that you have to tools to create a video, you need content. Wikipedia is an excellent source of copyright free content, you can use to create your videos. There are many keyword phrases that you can use to find material. Later on in this chapter you will learn how to use the Google Ad Planner to get the best keyword phrases to use in your videos.

YouTube Real Estate Marketing SEO – The Key to Internet Riches

Search Engine Optimization

Analytics: Video Viewership

Through out this chapter I am going to discuss many YouTube analytics that factor into how your video is ranked in YouTube. Once someone clicks onto your video to view it, YouTube keeps track of how many minutes it was view. Videos that are viewed from beginning to end get ranked higher base on the belief that the content is good because the viewer keeps watching it. For this reason, it is usually a good idea to keep most your videos under five minutes. In addition, this allows you to create more videos to a related topic. It is better to have twenty 3 minute videos than one 1 hour video, because it is more likely that the 3 minute videos will be watched in their entirety. Also by creating 20 videos you now have 20 possible places for AdSense to place monetized ads and thus increase your earning potential 20 times.

Tags, Keywords and Keyword Phrases

Tags, keywords and keyword phrases are the most important part of getting your YouTube video to rank on the first page of YouTube. There is an old saying..."If you commit murder, where do you hide the body, where nobody will find it? On the second page of Google".

YouTube Real Estate Marketing SEO – The Key to Internet Riches

Although we are working on YouTube the principle is the same. You must rank on the first page of YouTube in order for your video to get views from standard YouTube web site traffic.

Keywords are words that relate to your video. Some keywords for business are:

Business, Marketing and Start-up

Keyword Phrases for business are:

how to make money from home, internet marketing, small business grants

Tags are Keywords or Keyword Phrases that you place on your YouTube video's editing page, in order to get viewers to find your video.

Your goal is to try to rank in the top 20(land on the first page of YouTube) for every or most of the Tags in your video.

Your Video Title

The title of your video should be a keyword phrase that you want to rank for. It should also be relevant to the content in the video. When your title, tags and description are all relevant it boosts your YouTube rankings.

YouTube Real Estate Marketing
SEO – The Key to Internet Riches

Video Description

Each video is allowed to have a description. At the top of the description box, is where you should place a clickable or hyperlink, to either your web site or another video that you wish to viewer to see. Below the link should be a description of the video that contains content that is relative to the video. One short cut you can use it to cut and paste your video script into the description.

You video description should also have the keywords you used as tags. This adds to the videos relevancy.

You should also put links in you video to your social media addresses.

Half Time Adjustments

Any tags that are ranking your video in the top 20 should be placed in the headline/title of the video to boost their rank even higher.

One software that helps save you a tremendous amount of time doing this is called Tube Buddy.

https://www.tubebuddy.com/

YouTube Real Estate Marketing
Writing Your Script

CREATING CONTENT

You have two options for creating content. On screen video of yourself using a digital camera or phone camera. Take notes of what you will discuss.

Know your topic before you hit record.

Recording Tips:

* Use good lighting.

* Try recording near a window during the day time.

* Limit background noise as much as possible.

* Use a POWERPOINT screen capture style video.

* Create bullet points

* Use free software like jing or camstudio to record it. You can also get a free 30 day trial of camtasia from TechSmith

* www.screencast-o-matic.com is another free solution.

* Use your computer's built in microphone.

YouTube Real Estate Marketing
Writing Your Script

* Use a usb microphone is ideal, but not required.

* if you or kids have a usb gaming headset that works as well.

* most smart phones have a mp3 recording option.

Writing Your Script

Try to use words in your script that get and hold your viewers attention. Words like... you, want, now, free, limited time, All-American, imagine and how to, are just a few of the many words that are proven to stir a viewers emotions. Viewing a few copy writing videos on YouTube should help you to chose attention grabbing words.

AIDA is an acronym used in marketing and advertising that describes a common list of events that may occur when a consumer engages with an advertisement.

- A – attention (awareness): attract the attention of the customer.
- I – interest of the customer.
- D – desire: convince customers that they want and desire the product or service and that it will satisfy their needs.
- A – action: lead customers towards taking action and/or purchasing.

YouTube Real Estate Marketing
Writing Your Script

Using a system like this gives one a general understanding of how to target a market effectively. Moving from step to step, one loses some percent of prospects.

AIDA is a historical model, rather than representing current thinking in the methods of advertising effectiveness.

A basic rule of thumb for writing your script is that one paragraph equals about 60 seconds of talking. So if you are trying to shoot a 3 minute video you what to create a 3 paragraph document for your script. Try to use words in our script that are relevant to the title of your video.

You can also cut and paste your script into a YouTube video editor, and make your video Closed Captioned. This will increase your rankings in the YouTube search engine and it will allow more people to understand your video and increase your views.

CREATING TOPICS FOR YOUR VIDEOS

It is time to brainstorm and write down topics for your videos.

Remember you could choose a video around your own information product if you had it.

YouTube Real Estate Marketing
Writing Your Script

Get a notepad and think of 10 to 20 FAQ about your business.

http://answers.yahoo.com

Is a good source to find out what the potiential customers of your business are interested in.

Also look at articles on ezinearticles.com and see what topics come up the most for articles related to your business.

You can also browse forums related to your business.

Take a look at information products about your target market.

When you make a video that features Frequently Asked Questions each faq could be a short 1 to 3 minute video.

Use nichesuggest.com for a list of possible keyword ideas as well as seocentro and the google keyword planner.

Brainstorm 5 to 10 additional solution oriented videos. You should cover why the solution you are offering is better and why does your product recommendation solve your customer's problem.

YouTube Real Estate Marketing
Writing Your Script

Try to think of every advantage possible. Read other reviews of similar products or businesses or view sales pages for ideas of content for your videos.

Creating a Multipurpose Close

There are certain things that you should say in almost all of your videos:

* Thank the viewer for watching

* Ask the viewer to Thumbs up or Like your video

* Ask the viewer to subscribe to your YouTube Channel

* Ask the viewer to leave a comment

* Ask the viewer to share your video link with friends or social media

YouTube Real Estate Marketing
Writing Your Script

YOUR CALL TO ACTION

send your website visitors to a variety of places.

* A free website through weebly.com

* A free page through squidoo.com

* A free blog through blogspot.com

Use a tracking link like www.bit.ly or www.tinyurl.com

be careful as these links can change on you.

YouTube Real Estate Marketing
Writing Your Script

UPLOADING VIDEO

Create your account at www.youtube.com you can use a google account if you have one already created. Upload your video. Then provide your keyword rich video title. Look at other examples of videos performing well in that space. Use keywords from your niche or business and topic research write a good description with the keywords in it.

Try to include at least 2 sentences in your description. More content in your description will not hurt you. Include your website link at the beginning of the description use format http://www.yourfreelink.com encourage likes, comments, or honest feedback at the end of the description. Make a call to action in the description as well.

Chapter 12

Florida FL
Real Estate

State of Florida Overview

Florida is spanish for "land of flowers". One of the things that makes Florida a great place to be a real estate investor is that it has a population of 21,299,325 (2018 est.) the third highest in the United States! The Florida median household income is in the top 50 nationwide with $52,594, which is ranked number 40.

Other nice facts about Florida:

Spoken languages: Predominantly English and Spanish

Motto: In God We Trust

State song: Old Folks at Home

State Nickname: The Sunshine State

State Anthem: Where the Sawgrass Meets the Sky

State Capital: Tallahassee

Biggest city: Jacksonville

Biggest metro: Miami

Area: 65,757.70 sq mi

Ranked: 22 nationwide

State of Florida Overview

Any business person, especially a real estate investor, wants to have a business where the customer base has plenty of money. Another thing that makes Florida's a fantastic place to be an investor is it's $1.0 trillion economy. It is the fourth largest in the United States. If Florida was a country, it would be the 16th largest economy in the world, as well as the fifthty eighth most populous as of 2018. More great invesor numbers...In 2017, Florida's per capita personal income was $47,684, ranking 26th in the nation.

In 2018 Florida ranked 18th in the United States with an unemployment rate at only 3.5 percent.

The Miami economy has the 12th highest gross domestic product in the United States at $345 billion dollars.

Tampa Bay has the 2nd largest economy in the state with a gross domestic product of $145 billion dollars.

Is there money in Florida? Over fifty billionaires call the state of Florida home.

Florida has a high population growth and what seems to be, a never ending amount of new construction!

State of Florida Overview

Walt Disney World, Universal Studios, Busch Gardens and Fun Spot are just a handful of the amusement parks that help to drive the Florida economy. The state's economy also relies on agriculture, transportation, crops of oranges, and the Kennedy Space Center.

Florida is known all over the world as the place to be to play golf, tennis, and enjoy a ton of water sports. Several beaches in Florida have turquoise and emerald-colored coastal waters. Siesta Key beach in Florida made the Travel Channels list as one of the top beaches in the world. It has a 99 percent quartz base sand that remains cool to the touch and feels like baby power when walked on!

The year round warm weather makes Florida a popular destination for retirees.

As an investor, speaking spanish would give you a great business advantage as Florida has a large spanish speaking Latino community. But Florida is diverse with African, European, and indigenous heritage as part of it's landscape.

Find Florida Wholesale Real Estate Fast!

The internet has made it possible to grow your real estate investing business quickly and easily. Now you can view a hundred houses online without ever leaving your home.

In this chapter I am going to give you a ton of web sites and the addresses to government wholesale sources, to help you to cover this state's real estate goldmines. I have selected some of the biggest counties with the largest supply of wholesale real estate.

In general you should look at 100 homes for every 1 property that you purchase. Comparing factors like the home value, rent potential, repair cost, local taxes, possible home owner fees, utilities etc...

While there is no substitute for inspecting a home in person, having access to thousands of homes on the internet can help you to narrow down the field to spectacular deals! So take advantage of this knowledge to help secure your real estate investing success!

Find Florida Wholesale Real Estate Fast!

Locate Statewide Florida Properties

MLS.com

This web site has Florida Real Estate Foreclosures with links to different cities on the landing page.

http://www.mls.com/search/florida.mvc

REALTOR.com

This web site has Links to Florida real estate properties by county and city.

http://www.realtor.com/foreclosures/Florida

Top Florida Counties

The previous web sites give you access to a broad selection of property in all 67 counties in Florida.

Next I narrow it down to a handful of the top counties based on the population size, rising property values, rental profit potential and the abundance of wholesale property available.

Find Florida Wholesale Real Estate Fast!

Miami-Dade County

Miami-Dade County has a population of 2,662,874 and is 1,946 square miles. The best Goldmine investment oppurtunities in this county are Miami and Hialeah.

Delinquent Taxes and Tax Certificate Sales

Miami-Dade County Tax Collector

140 West Flagler St., 1st Floor, Suite 1407, Miami, FL 33130

Phone: (305) 375-5452

Tax Certificate Information:

https://urlzs.com/StaQr

Auction Web site:

https://bidmiamidade.com/

Tax Deed Sales:

https://urlzs.com/nsPcP

Find Florida Wholesale Real Estate Fast!

Broward County

Broward County has a population of 1,780,172 and is 1,209 square miles. The best Goldmine real estate investment oppurtunities in this county are Fort Lauderdale.

Delinquent Taxes and Tax Certificate Sales

Broward County Revenue Collector

Broward County Governmental Center Annex

115 South Andrews Avenue, Fort Lauderdale, FL 33301

Phone: (954)831-4000

Foreclosure Sales

https://www.broward.realforeclose.com/index.cfm

Tax Deed

https://broward.deedauction.net/

Tax Lien

https://www.bidbroward.com/

Find Florida Wholesale Real Estate Fast!

Hillsborough County

Hillsborough County has a population of 1,267,775 and is 1,051 square miles. The best Goldmine real estate investment oppurtunities in this county are in Tampa.

Tax Certificate Sales

Hillsborough County Tax Collector
601 E. Kennedy Blvd., 14th Floor, Tampa, FL 33602
Phone: (813) 635-5200 Fax: (813) 612-6707

Foreclosure:

https://www.hillsborough.realforeclose.com/index.cfm

Tax Deed Sale Information:

https://urlzs.com/rrKtU

Find Florida Wholesale Real Estate Fast!

Orange County

Orange County has a population of 1,169,107 and is 908 square miles. The best Goldmine real estate investment oppurtunities in this county are in Orlando.

Orange County Tax Collector
200 South Orange Ave., Suite 1500, Orlando, FL 32802
Phone: (407) 836-2700

Government Foreclosures:

https://www.myorangeclerk.realforeclose.com/index.cfm

Tax Sales:

http://www.octaxcol.com/tax-certificate-deed-sales/

https://www.occompt.com/official-records/tax-deed-sales/

Find Florida Wholesale Real Estate Fast!

Pinellas County

Pinellas County has a population of 917,398 and is 280 square miles. The best Goldmine real estate investment oppurtunities in this county are in Petersburg.

Pinellas County Tax Collector
29399 US Highway 19 N, Suite 100, Clearwater, FL 33761
Phone: (727) 464-7777

Government Foreclosures:

https://www.pinellas.realforeclose.com/

Tax Sales:

https://taxcollect.com/tax-certificate-deed-sales/

Find Florida Wholesale Real Estate Fast!

Duval County

Duval County has a population of 870,709 and is 918 square miles. The best Goldmine real estate investment oppurtunities in this county are in Jacksonville.

Duval County Tax Collector
231 E. Forsyth St., Jacksonville, FL 32202
Phone: (904) 630-1916

Government Foreclosures:

https://www.duval.realforeclose.com/

Tax Sales:

https://duvalfl.realtaxlien.com/

Find Florida Wholesale Real Estate Fast!

Lee County

Lee County has a population of 631,330 and is 804 square miles. The best Goldmine real estate investment oppurtunities in this county are in **Cape Coral**.

Lee County Tax Collector
2480 Thompson St., Fort Myers, FL 33902
Phone: (239) 533-6000

Government Foreclosures:

https://www.lee.realforeclose.com/index.cfm

Florida Real Estate Investing

City Goldmines

1. Jacksonville

The city of Jacksonville has a population of 867,313 to support your real estate investing business.

The **median home value** in Jacksonville is $177,500. Jacksonville is a real estate goldmine city because recently the home values have gone up 8 percent and is expected to rise at least another 4 percent.

Houses currently listed in Jacksonville have a median list price of about $220,000. Homes that actually sold have a median price of about $160,000.

The **median rent price** in Jacksonville is about $1300. This ranks #6 between Florida Goldmine Cities.

Foreclosure Warning sign

Delinquent mortgages in Jacksonville is 1.9 percent. The *Foreclosure potiential rank is #1 between Florida goldmine cities.*

Florida Real Estate Investing

City Goldmines

2. Miami

The city of Miami has a population of 443,007 to support your real estate investing business.

The **median home value** in Miami is $337.200. Miami is a real estate goldmine city because recently the home values have gone up 2.8 percent and is expected to rise at least another 0.4 percent.

Houses currently listed in Miami have a median list price of about $475,000. Homes that actually sold have a median price of about $312,000.

The **median rent price** in Miami is about $2,430. This ranks #1 between Florida Goldmine Cities.

Foreclosure Warning sign

Delinquent mortgages in Miami is 1.2 percent. The *Foreclosure potiential rank is #6 between Florida goldmine cities.*

Florida Real Estate Investing

City Goldmines

3. Tampa

The city of Tampa has a population of 368,087 to support your real estate investing business.

The median home value in Tampa is $221,100. Tampa is a real estate goldmine city because recently the home values have gone up 5.5 percent and is expected to rise at least another 1.6 percent.

Houses currently listed in Tampa have a median price of about $335,000. Homes that actually sold have a median list price of about $214,000.

The median rent price in Tampa is about $1,600. This ranks #4 between Florida Goldmine Cities.

Foreclosure Warning sign

Delinquent mortgages in Tampa is 1.3 percent. The *Foreclosure potiential rank is #4 between Florida goldmine cities.*

Florida Real Estate Investing

City Goldmines

4. Orlando

The city of Orlando has a population of 269,414 to support your real estate investing business.

The median home value in Orlando is $241,200. Orlando is a real estate goldmine city because recently the home values have gone up 6.7 percent and is expected to rise at least another 2.8 percent.

Houses currently listed in Orlando have a median price of about $290,000. Homes that actually sold have a median list price of about $248,000.

The median rent price in Orlando is about $1,600. This ranks #4 between Florida Goldmine Cities.

Foreclosure Warning sign

Delinquent mortgages in Orlando is 1.2 percent. The *Foreclosure potiential rank is #6 between Florida goldmine cities.*

Florida Real Estate Investing

City Goldmines

5. Hialeah

The city of Hialeah has a population of 237,523 to support your real estate investing business.

The median home value in Hialeah is $286,300. Hialeah is a real estate goldmine city because recently the home values have gone up 8.4 percent and is expected to rise at least another 3.0 percent.

Houses currently listed in Hialeah have a median price of about $319,950. Homes that actually sold have a median list price of about $253,000.

The median rent price in Hialeah is about $2,000. This ranks #2 between Florida Goldmine Cities.

Foreclosure Warning sign

Delinquent mortgages in Hialeah is 1.3 percent. The *Foreclosure potiential rank is #4 between Florida goldmine cities.*

Florida Real Estate Investing

City Goldmines

6. Tallahassee

The city of Tallahassee has a population of 188,463 to support your real estate investing business.

The median home value in Tallahassee is $183,400. Tallahassee is a real estate goldmine city because recently the home values have gone up 6.9 percent and is expected to rise at least another 2.8 percent.

Houses currently listed in Tallahassee have a median price of about $225,000. Homes that actually sold have a median list price of about $189,100.

The median rent price in Tallahassee is about $1,100. This ranks #7 between Florida Goldmine Cities.

Foreclosure Warning sign

Delinquent mortgages in Tallahassee is 1.4 percent. The *Foreclosure potiential rank is #3 between Florida goldmine cities.*

Florida Real Estate Investing

City Goldmines

7. Port St. Lucie

The city of Port St. Lucie has a population of 178,778 to support your real estate investing business.

The median home value in Port St. Lucie is $222,500. Port St. Lucie is a real estate goldmine city because recently the home values have gone up 7.0 percent and is expected to rise at least another 3.0 percent.

Houses currently listed in Port St. Lucie have a median price of about $247,000. Homes that actually sold have a median list price of about $211,000.

The median rent price in Port St. Lucie is about

$10,000

Massive Money Internet Marketing &

Copy Writing & SEO Course &

$1,000 Value Bonus

Internet Marketing Videos

LIBRARY I (Video Training Programs)

1. Product Creation
2. Copy Writing & Payment
3. Auto Responder & Product Download Page
4. How to start a Freelancing business
5. Video Marketing
6. List Building
7. Affiliate Marketing
8. How to Get Massive Web Site Traffic

LIBRARY II (Video Training Programs)

1. Goldmine Government Grants
2. How to Write a Business Plan
3. Secrets to making money on eBay
4. Credit Repair
5. Goal Setting
6. Asset Protection How to Incorporate

$10,000 MegaSized Internet Marketing &

Copy Writing & SEO Course &

$1,000 Value Bonus

Library III

1. SEO SIMPLIFIED PART 1

2. SEO SIMPLIFIED PART 2

3. SEO Private Network Blogs

4. SEO Social Signals

5. SEO Profits

Bonus 1000 Package!

1. Insider Secrets to Government Contracts (PDF)

2. 1000 Books/Guides (text files)

3. Vacation Discounts (text file w/links to discounts)

4. Media Players (3 Software Programs)

100% MONEY BACK GUARANTEE!!!

ALL ON A 8 GIGABYTE FLASH DRIVE

This Massive Library with a $10,000 value all for only a
1 time payment of $67!!!

Get Instant Access by Using the Link Below:

https://urlzs.com/p7v3T

Leave a review and join Our VIP Mailing List Then Get All our Audio Books Free! We will be releasing over 100 money making audio books within the next 12 months! Just leave a review and join our mailing list and get them all for free!

Just Hit/Type in the Link Below

https://urlzs.com/HfbGF

www.ingramcontent.com/pod-product-compliance
Lightning Source LLC
Chambersburg PA
CBHW071658210326
41597CB00017B/2235